Memory Lane

Cambridge

Cambridge Evening News
The Award Winning — Voice of Mid-Anglia

Memory Lane • Cambridge

Mike Petty

The Breedon Books
Publishing Company
Derby

First published in Great Britain by
The Breedon Books Publishing Company Limited
Breedon House, 44 Friar Gate, Derby, DE1 1DA.
1999

ISBN 1 85983 184 2

Printed and bound by Butler & Tanner Ltd., Selwood Printing Works,
Caxton Road, Frome, Somerset.

Colour separations and jacket printing by Green Shires Group Ltd,
Leicester.

Contents

Foreword

The very mention of the name Cambridge around the world conjures up pictures of a university city steeped in history.

It's an image that everyone connected with Cambridge is so rightly proud of. However, there is much more to our city and this book has been produced to help readers capture some wonderful memories.

Michael Petty, local author, historian and former curator of the Cambridgeshire Collection, has compiled a book which traces the post-war years in Cambridge.

It is a fascinating documentation – in pictures and words – of an era that saw remarkable changes and progress.

We thank everyone who has played a part in bringing the book together and hope you enjoy this splendid publication.

Colin Grant
Editor
Cambridge Evening News
September 1999

Introduction

In 1963 the *Cambridge News*, as it then was, launched a major new series of feature articles entitled *Down Your Street*. Its compiler, Erica Dimock, talked to residents and traders from one end of the town to the other, recording their opinions and making her own assessment of the areas she visited at that time. Her articles were accompanied by specially-taken photographs. Together they presented a view of modern, 1960s Cambridge, which time has turned to memories.

Those pictures and the words she wrote form part of this nostalgic look back at Cambridge over the last 40 years.

They have been supplemented by other pictures taken by Cedric Tarrant, Eddie Collinson, Mick Manni, Tony Jedrej, Dave Parfitt, Chris Bouchier, Paul Craske, Chis Morton and other *News* photographers. They have collectively compiled the most comprehensive pictorial record anywhere of life in post-war Cambridge in all its complexity.

I have tried where possible to locate the actual captions that accompanied the pictures when they were first published, and these are recorded in quotation marks. The opinions are thus those of the time, expressing the hopes and fears of the period.

Other information has come from *News* readers who have responded to my appeals for assistance in my recent "Memories" columns.

For their patience while I have plundered their files, and their ready assistance whenever I asked for it, I am most grateful to the *News* library staff.

While I may regret the rebuilding of the old Petty Cury, the disappearance of small shops, the loss of communities where everybody knew everyone, let us not forget the comfort of central heating, of hot water on tap, modern amenities – and those in modern Cambridge who do not enjoy them.

Inevitably, there will be things that have been forgotten that you would wish to have had remembered, pictures taken over the years which have not made their way into the *News* library files, more memories than can be crammed into the current book. Please continue to share them through the pages of the *Cambridge Evening News* for, as this selection makes clear, today has a habit of becoming history very quickly!

Mike Petty
September 1999

The City Centre

Market Hill during a brief encounter with winter in mid-December 1974. The snow had gone within the hour and only this *News* photograph remains to recall the scene.

Cambridge comes alive at night: youngsters and their night-time motorbikes outside Burton's in September 1963. Beyond are the International Stores and Otto Wehrle's jewellers, both now just memories. When Eddie Wehrle closed his premises in April 1970, it ended a 125-year trading link with, at one time, four shops. The clock itself was taken down but later renovated and returned to Market Hill in September 1986.

The east side of Market Hill, seen from an upper room in the Guildhall, in September 1969. Councillors were debating the future layout of the market which seemed to be in decline. Some proposed grouping all the stalls at one end to allow the other free for parking. In the event parking was banned completely and stalls spread right across Market Hill.

By 1990, when a victorious Cambridge United toured the city having won promotion to the Third Division by beating Chesterfield 1-0 at Wembley Stadium, there had been various changes. Eastern Electricity had expanded their showrooms into Wehrle's old shop. Marks and Spencer had opened, replacing both the Victoria cinema and Freeman Hardy and Willis shoe shop.

Cinema goers leave the Victoria having witnessed Cambridge's first all-night horror film show in November 1972. More than 600 people witnessed Dracula, Frankenstein, vampires and bodysnatchers, sustained only by hot-dogs and soft drinks between 11.30pm and 8am. And nobody died of shock. The cinema had started life as the Electric Theatre in 1911, being renamed Victoria in 1915. It moved to the site shown here in 1931. In 1952 the cinema had been redesigned in a "eurythmic" style "designer, architect and illuminators combining to make a symphony of shape, colour and tone". It closed in January 1988.

Mayor Peter Warren, MP Sir Hamilton Kerr and Sergeant at Mace Ken Quick, amongst others, process to Great St Mary's Church for a Corporation service on Armistice Day 1964. The sermon was preached by Pastor Neimuller, a German "U-boat" commander turned parson. The dignitaries then returned to the Guildhall for sherry.

Mayor Horace Ives on the Guildhall balcony with a delegation of athletes from Cambridge's twin city, Heidelberg, in June 1965. In the background a line of parked cars stretches down Petty Cury.

Guildhall and the corner of Petty Cury, 14 October 1964. The shops are Sketchley's cleaners, Morley's wine bar, Dolamore's wines and spirits, Finlay the tobacconist and Heffer's bookshop.

Heffer's bookshop, October 1964. It had first opened in Petty Cury in 1896, and moved to a new shop in Trinity Street in 1970 in advance of Lion Yard redevelopment.

An alleyway beside Heffer's provided a useful place for displaying bargain books and storing bicycles. It led to a fine Georgian house providing offices for Ellison & Co, solicitors, photographed here in May 1962.

A dog slumbers in Petty Cury on a September evening in 1963, keeping guard on parked cars outside the illuminated sign of the Lion Hotel. The Lion had closed all but its bars in March 1963 and was demolished in 1968.

A "To Let" sign hangs over premises previously occupied by Lipton's, in this October 1964 picture. Beyond Falcon Yard was Mac Fisheries with a large live fish tank under its display counter that fascinated generations of children, and Hunts dress shop.

Hunts was replaced by John Barry. Across Alexandra Street was Dewhurst the butcher, John Collier's tailor, Alexandre of Oxford Street, Dipple and Conway opticians, Separates – the first Cambridge shop specifically to sell sweaters and skirts rather than complete dresses – and the Civic Restaurant. The gap in the street where the Lion Hotel once stood presages the demolition that was soon to follow.

Time for tea – or Fanta, sausage and beans. Inside the Civic Restaurant, October 1968. In April 1961 it was preparing family meals for over 1,000 people a day for consumption in its spacious contemporary dining room, for the Drummer Street mobile canteen or the WVS Meals on Wheels service. By 1966 it was making a handsome profit. It closed at the end of March 1972 in the run-up to the Lion Yard redevelopment.

The north side of Petty Cury, seen from the corner of Sidney Street in October 1964 showing True Form shoes, Dunn & Co outfitters, Hepworth's tailors, H. Samuel's jeweller and Boots the Chemist.

"The charm of old and narrow streets is ruined when traffic and shoppers mix," commented the *News* in June 1964. Not the time for window shopping at Dixon's cameras, especially if you have the children with you. Cars, lorries and buses continued to trundle down Petty Cury until pedestrianisation in 1972.

Falcon Yard looking under the archway to the Dixon's sign in Petty Cury, 1964. People remember Mac Fisheries on the corner, but forget the smell of Billingsgate that lingered around the area.

Alexandra Street in March 1961 when it was home to Cook's fruit shop, Pigott's printers, the Hang Chow Chinese Restaurant, Henekey's wine bar – a very popular watering hole – and the Citizens' Advice Bureau.

In 1972 demolition men moved in to start the clearance for the new Lion Yard redevelopment. The YMCA in the background had provided generations of youngsters with entertainment of various types. In 1967 its old cellars were converted to a discotheque and club to add to the TV room, billiards, lounge, table tennis and restaurant. But by 1970 it had become "a rather dingy and inadequate place". A new building opened in Gonville Place in 1974.

Around the corner from the YMCA was the Alley Boutique. Its first shop opened in Falcon Yard in 1966, shortly after the Pussycat Boutique had pioneered in Cambridge the fashion craze that was sweeping the country. Alley 2 opened in 1968 to cater "from teeny boppers to swingin' mums" who bought dresses priced from £5 to £8. The shop moved to King Street until returning to Lion Yard when the new development was complete.

Demolition in July 1972 gives a glimpse back to the shops in Petty Cury – Boots, Dixons, Van Allan of London, ladies outfitters, Joe Lyon's café which closed in 1974, Dolcis shoes and Dewhurst. The YMCA and building which once housed the Bell Telephone Company await their fate.

The bulldozers breaks through to St Andrew's Street in November 1972, giving a glimpse behind it of the new Lion Yard multi-storey car park which had been opened earlier that year.

The whole complex was opened by Princess Anne on 4 December 1975, here escorted by the Mayor, Councillor R. May, and Councillor Peter Wright, chairman of the Central Developments Action Panel. The scheme had been designed by Arup Associates with Fewster & Partners as executive architects and Bovis as main contractors.

Thousands gathered on Market Hill in June 1993, to see Diana, Princess of Wales, accompanied by Mayor Alex MacEachern. She had previously toured the University's Physiological Laboratory and moved on to Papworth Hospital.

Though just steps away from Lion Yard the princess resisted the temptation to visit its shops – seen here in November 1980.

Although if the Alley Boutique and Waits had continued to trade either side of the Golden Egg, as here in 1975 perhaps… Lion Yard has seen a continual change of tenants and in 1999 plans neared fruition for a remodelling of the centre, and indeed for a new arcade which might replace the Lion Yard car park – which itself may become but a memory.

Around the Centre

The Red Cow on the corner of Corn Exchange Street was originally scheduled for demolition as part of the Lion Yard redevelopment. Instead it was renovated and the pub extended into sections which in 1964 housed Abbott's tourist centre and Precision watch repairs.

The Corn Exchange alongside provided an all-purpose venue – including this 1965 motor show when a prototype Triumph GT6 is displayed, third right and, more exotic still a Volvo P1800 "The Saint's" car, displayed by Harston Motors.

The Corn Exchange was converted to a concert hall in 1987. Before that it had acted as a multi-functional venue for dances, wrestling matches and roller skating, as here in October 1974. The *News* for May 1970 reported as many as 200 young people regularly crowded into the Corn Exchange to take advantage of evening skating sessions. At 2s (10p), skating was cheaper than the cinema and besides there was "nowhere to go on Monday". Roller skating stopped at the Corn Exchange in April 1982 and continued at the Kelsey Kerridge sports hall. But by then the youngsters were into skateboarding, with a skateboard park opening at Cheddar's Lane in 1978, and closing the next year.

Looking across Lion Yard just before full-scale redevelopment began. Many of the old buildings behind the Lion Hotel had been cleared to make a car park; landmarks in the background include St John's College chapel tower, Holy Trinity Church and the spire of All Saints' Church in Jesus Lane.

Traffic in Downing Street junction with St Tibbs' Row in December 1969. The Bun Shop public house in the background carried a date of 1902 on its chimney. "Scores of people still flock there to enjoy friendly and lively hospitality. Two rooms are served by one bar and its lofty walls are decorated by three enormous murals by J. Hamilton. It is not tarted up and few places are left in town with such character," said the *Romsey Town News* in December 1974 shortly before the pub's demolition.

The imposing Edwardian Norwich Union building at the junction of Downing Street and St Andrew's Street was replaced in 1970.

Evening traffic in St Andrew's Street negotiates the bottle-neck at the corner of Downing Street as demolition of the Norwich Union building gets under way, 1970.

Queues form outside Vogue fashion shop, just down the street, for its closing down sale in December 1983. It specialised in clothes from the 12 leading London fashion houses.

More bargains to be had at the Belfast Linen Warehouse Great Winter sale in 1963. Double quilts were down from 79s 11d (£3.99) to 67s 11d (£3.40), while Sun-aire blinds would make your windows gay! The store was established in Regent Street, Cambridge, in 1905, moving to St Andrew's Street three years later where it continued to trade until March 1998.

Tesco opened its first store in Cambridge just beyond the old police station in 1964 and soon attracted crowds of shoppers. It closed in 1983 after the opening of its store in Bar Hill.

One shop that has survived is Robert Sayle, seen quiet on this Saturday afternoon in 1966, with plenty of parking outside and even traffic wardens find little to do – perhaps it had something to do with a World Cup Final match between England and West Germany. In 1999 came plans for a major redevelopment and new arcade stretching back to Lion Yard.

Bradwell's Court, Cambridge's first modern shopping arcade, opened in 1961. Christ's Lane, the previous thoroughfare from Drummer Street, closed and Roe's antique shop moved to Downing Street. The arcade was photographed here in October 1964.

Drummer Street bus station, November 1978. The lime trees rising high over the central island site were the sole survivors of a battle fought when the bus station was carved from Christ's Pieces. It was remodelled in 1985 and again in 1991 but is still the centre of debate.

The old central shelter provided "a chance to rest weary legs and have a bite before the bus comes", December 1970. Nearby a man would watch your bags whilst you continued shopping.

Lloyds Bank, Sidney Street, seen across the rubble of the Lion Yard redevelopment site in August 1972.

Sidney Street seen from the corner of Petty Cury in June 1964. Like much of the rest of central Cambridge it had been redeveloped in the 1930s although there had been changes to the Boots frontage in 1960, a time which also saw the arrival of the Wallis fashion shop.

A damp evening on the run-up to Christmas 1984, the Christmas lights competing with those of Marks and Spencer who arrived in the street in 1934.

Shop assistants Barbara Wilson and Maureen Stratton in Marks and Spencer, July 1966, when foam interlined Bri-nylon bras cost 7s 11d (39p).

Crowds outside Sainsbury's shop, 17 Sidney Street, on a wet April day in 1961. The firm opened a new supermarket further along the street in 1972 as part of a policy to replace service stores. Note the police phone box.

On the corner of Market Street and Sidney Street, Joshua Taylor attracted large crowds for their sales. Here, a queue builds up at from the building until it closed in April 1996.

From the police box PC Martin Jenkins notifies control that five-year-old David Ward is safe in the hands of PC Jim Pike, July 1973. Mum was found a few minutes later.

Eaden Lilley's shop in Market Street, September 1966. The firm remodelled the premises, reopening in September 1993 but closed in June 1999 after nearly 250 years. The shop was bought by the US firm Borders, the second largest book retailers in the world.

8.47am just after Christmas 1987. The family firm sold up in 1991 after 130 years' trading. Various franchises continued to operate

Market Street in June 1964 when Joshua Taylor, Achille Serre cleaners, Eaden Lilley and Jarrold's were amongst those trading. Scaffolding in the background marks the rebuilding of the former site of Mackintosh's shop.

Another name that has disappeared is the Dorothy whose premises included a Continental delicatessen and supermarket – there was a special offer on Heinz condensed soups for 1s (5p) in October 1963.

The Dorothy is better remembered for its restaurant and ballroom where tea dances were held until 1963 and many other functions continued until its closure in August 1972. Here some of the 1,100 employees and guests who enjoyed themselves at the Cambridge and District Co-operative Society's staff party about 1967.

One entrance to the Dorothy was in Hobson Street, just across the passageway from the Central cinema, which converted to a bingo hall in 1972.

Sussex Street was another product of inter-war redevelopment, photographed in 1964 when it was home to Roper's tailors, Easiphit footwear, Gordon Thoday drapers, Rose's Fashion Centre, New Bon, Lewis of Westminster tobacconist, Morley and Duke electricians, Ridgeon's seeds, W.H. Peak floor covering specialists, Paris House costumiers, and Granta wool stores.

Piggot's tool shop was also in Sidney Street. Here shop assistant F.C. Woods waits for customers in its centenary year 1963; the shop closed in 1984.

Just around the corner is King Street, famous in student terms for the King Street Run – an undergraduate competition which required sinking a pint of beer in each of its pubs in the shortest possible time.

"A winding street of ancient cottages, strangely inconsistent with its situation in the heart of a University city, King Street has a charm and quaintness carefully preserved by those who live and work in it. Famous for its superfluity of public houses, and well-known for its miscellany of small, individual businesses, it is a street which may become a password for motorists anxiously seeking parking space close to the commercial and historic centre of Cambridge," said the *News* in March 1963.

"King Street may not have been great architecture, but it is sickening indeed to see it give way to inhumanity and chaos; a commercial backwater, it had been saved from the pressure which disfigured the busier streets. Who would have guessed that it survived only to fall victim to the no-less disfiguring pressure of the academic world and its distinguished architects," wrote the *Architectural Review* in 1972, commenting on the new Christ's College development. It was later softened by rebuilding.

Jesus Lane. "…now a very busy thoroughfare, a favourite spot for motorists to park their cars and the home of collegiate buildings with world-wide reputation. The houses retain some of their dignity, but whether this will be so when the routes of relief roads for Cambridge have finally been decided, no one can tell," said the *News* in April 1963. The old Friends' Meeting House on the corner of Park Street was replaced by a new building in 1969.

Lord Butler, Master of Trinity College, took on the role of cashier to serve Lady Butler at the new Trustee Savings Bank in Jesus Lane which opened in January 1967.

Looking down Bridge Street from the junction with Jesus Lane, showing King and Harper car premises on the right.

By 1964 there were proposals for the demolition of the old buildings on the corner of Bridge Street and Round Church Street which were crumbling and in a bad state of repair. Instead they were restored and reopened as a "landmark and inspiration" in April 1977.

However, buildings in Ram Yard, including Prziborsky's hairdressing shop, were removed in 1961 to provide access to the new multi-storey car park in Park Street.

Portugal Place was home to Jack Carter, robe maker, who hired gowns, tails and dinner suits to students and townsfolk from 1937. The business closed in 1981. Nearby Joshua Taylor made a large proportion of the robes worn in universities, councils and courts throughout Britain and the Commonwealth. In 1965 they produced the coronation robes for the King and Queen of Tonga, here modelled by Norman Douglas who, not having the stature of Tonga's monarch, was actually standing on a box!

Portugal Place remains one of the attractive Cambridge back streets, dominated by St John's College Chapel and covered in snow, February 1970.

A street further north, Thompson's Lane houses were dominated by the chimney of the electricity generating station in Quay Side when this picture was taken in January 1964. Then "the generating station can produce 7,000 kilowatts per hour. This is augmented by two nearby transformers which are connected to the grid system and supply the whole of Cambridge. But the amount from the generating station is in fact only used at peak periods".

The electricity works seen in the background closed in 1966 and were demolished in 1982, since when the area has been comprehensively developed. Here snow is tipped into the river in January 1963 apparently swamping the punt-hirer's boat.

A telephoto lens compresses the city centre in August 1968. Landmarks, from the distance, include Spiller's flour mills at the station, the Roman Catholic church, St Paul's and St Edward's Church towers, the tapering tops of Lloyd's Bank and the Round Church. In the centre is the tower of St Clement's Church and the curved roof of the building at the entrance to St John's Street.

Magdalene Bridge was subjected to a weight restriction of 12 tons, reducing the amount of heavy traffic across it. The bridge was rebuilt and reopened in 1982.

Bridge Street continued to provide a traffic route into the centre of the city until it was closed to most vehicles in January 1997.

Cambridge's last thatched cottage in Clement Place, off Bridge Street, pictured here in May 1961, was demolished in 1972.

The junction of Bridge Street and St John's Street, July 1964, the Corner House hairdressing saloon offering Marcel and Permanent waving for ladies and children.

Matthew's grocery shop in Trinity Street closed in May 1964 after 134 years. "One cannot offer a traditional grocery service from a large city centre site at present rental values," they claimed. A little later Sainsbury's opened in Sidney Street.

A traffic warden patrols Trinity Street; the Turk's Head Grill closed in 1978 and the Blue Boar Hotel in 1986. In the background is the relocated Heffer's bookshop which opened in October 1970; in 1999 they sold their business to Blackwells of Oxford.

On the other side of the street these fashion-conscious bargain hunters are queuing for Arthur Shepherd's clothing sale in December 1965. During the 1950s the proprietor, Geoffrey Smith, took advantage of the end of wartime rationing to introduce narrow-legged trousers – he disliked the term "drainpipes". The shop originally catered for discerning undergraduates but following the student revolution in dress of the late 1960s, they cultivated a more general trade.

Wrays Court, a picturesque area of "old Cambridge" photographed in February 1964 when it provided central homes for young families. It was demolished for the new Sainsbury's supermarket in Sidney Street.

In Green Street "the sound of the bookbinder's hammer and the scurrying of undergraduate feet on their way to college or lectures have long since been enveloped by the sound of motor cars (or in this case by fire engines in 1964) but in the mind's eye at least, the charm of Green Street, its institutions and personalities, will always remain," wrote the *News* in August 1963. In 1999 the street was remodelled to enhance its charm.

Visitors' and residents' cars clog King's Parade in October 1977. After various schemes the street was closed to traffic in 1981; 1999 saw an enhancement of the street layout.

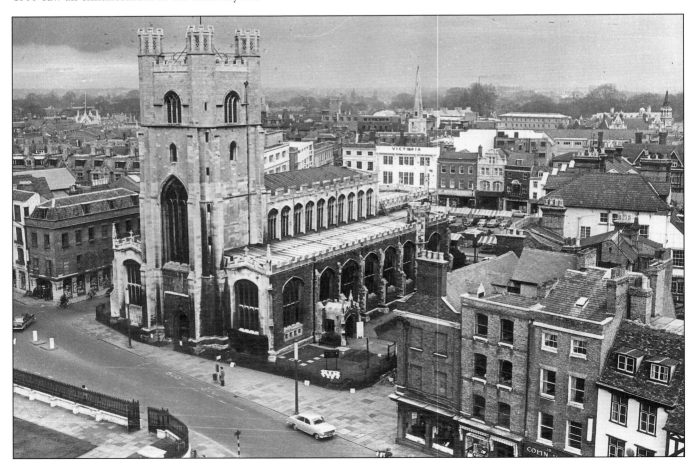

It is unlikely that cars will ever again sweep into St Mary's Street – a view from the top of Kings College Chapel *c.*1966.

Bene't Street from King's Parade in July 1964. A refurbished Eagle Inn opened in place of Hockey's estate agents in 1992.

Peas Hill, once the site of the fish market, was the site of controversy when the old Central Hotel was replaced by a new hostel for King's College in 1959. When this photograph was taken in 1964, Adkin's gave Green Shield Stamps and F.O. Sennitt's butcher's delivery bicycle was propped up outside their shop.

The Second Centre – the Kite area

Christ's Pieces: its tree-lined walk was threatened in July 1966 by new plans for new roads; the plans were rejected and the trees survived until they were condemned and felled in November 1998.

Across Emmanuel Road, the New Square car park – seen here in February 1963 and which itself had been open space until 1932 – was restored to grass as part of the redevelopment of the Kite area.

The grass area mentioned in the previous caption leads to Cambridge's second shopping centre, dominated by the Laurie and McConnal store, its bandstand an imposing feature over Fitzroy Street seen here in June 1964. "In the past it used to be regarded as a rather poor shopping area with many of the stores dealing in cheap imported goods. In recent years, however, the situation has considerably changed and most of the traders in this part of Cambridge take great pride in what they have to sell." the *News* reported.

Looking along Fitzroy Street in June 1964. "Originating from the early 19th century and for many years one of the busiest streets in Cambridge, Fitzroy Street today is in the process of regaining some of its former importance. Parking and traffic difficulties in the town centre and the building of modern stores in the street have attracted many people to its shopping area," said the *News* on 11 June 1964.

The view down Burleigh Street in May 1970. On the left is the Eden Baptist Chapel, Laing's boots and shoe repairs, and James Smith's cleaners; on the right the Forester's pub, sub-Post Office and the Co-op.

"Boasting no buildings of historical or architectural interest and no special industries or associations, Burleigh Street's main claim to importance must be the fact that for nearly 100 years it has been the home of the Cambridge Co-operative Society. For the rest it is lined with small shops which provide a variety of merchandise for customers living in the area and for those avoiding the more stringent parking restrictions in the city centre" (*News* 27 August 1964). The Co-op sold off their lease in 1989 and closed their remaining foodstore in 1996.

Looking back along Burleigh Street from East Road, 22 June 1978, with the junction with Adam and Eve Street on the left. Despite the arrival of yellow lines, the emphasis was still on the ease of parking: "One of the easiest places for finding parking spaces – particularly at weekends. There are three large car parks – two in Gold Street and the other at New Square, and parking either at meters or just by the kerbside is widely permitted in the area's streets", (*News*).

The car park in Adam and Eve Street, June 1964.

Rebuilding work in Burleigh Street, opposite Adam and Eve Street, looking towards East Road, June 1964.

Elsewhere there was uncertainty over the future of the area, especially in the upper reaches of Fitzroy Street, seen here in June 1964. The Old English Gentleman pub offered a garden for the children, music at weekends and accommodation. Nearby was Fitzroy Motors and A.E. Stearn's wholesale grocers.

An old shop at the corner of Wellington Street. Such derelict properties were cleared as residents moved out to new homes on the Arbury estate.

In old church buildings in Wellington Street, the Cambridge Freebooters' coffee bar and youth club provided a meeting place for youngsters between the summer of 1960 and December 1962. The club was started by John Ewen, a theology student at Ridley Hall. Gradually they built up a remarkable atmosphere, organised film shows, and debated taboo subjects – such as birth control. It offered local 15 to 18-year-olds a unique experience and was strictly soft-drinks only.

Baldrey's soft drinks factory started in Gold Street in 1923. By 1969 they had taken over Barker and Wadsworth and could produce 800 dozen bottles of mineral water an hour, employing 25 people on two production lines. They relocated to Harvest Way, off Newmarket Road, in 1969, and to Sawston in 1979.

Old advertising signs in Fitzroy Street in November 1965 including that of the Little Kettle. "Next to Cartwright's former barber's shop, which closed down some time ago, is a hardware and grocery shop run by Mrs A.M. Verlander. A rather charming little kettle hangs outside. Mrs Verlander says that business is nothing like as busy as it used to be. 'People tend to forget this stretch of Fitzroy Street exists.' A new business started up recently across the road but moved elsewhere in a very short space of time because they got so little trade along here". The *News*, June 1964.

In days gone by, many Cambridge people would say: "If you can't get what you want at Verlander's, you won't get it at all". A scheme operated by the shop was really a forerunner of today's trading stamps. The Verlanders gave away coupons with the soap they sold and these could be exchanged for free gifts.

From the rear of the Little Kettle, Fitzroy Street, the scale of the dereliction is clear in December 1970.

The Little Kettle property came to symbolise opposition to comprehensive redevelopment of the area – Virginia La Charite with a proposal for its renovation by the Kite Co-ordinating Committee in March 1978. It was finally demolished in July 1981.

"Uninspiring in appearance, City Road is nevertheless one of the most controversial streets in Cambridge. It has changed very little this century but is now awaiting decisions which will not only have a great effect on City Road itself, but will determine the future of the whole of Cambridge. Demolition signs are a warning of things to come and the uncertainty of the future is making life in City Road a little difficult," said the *News* in March 1964. Here City Council planners make a survey of the area, seeking opinions in City Road, March 1973.

Fair Street, looking to New Square, an area of uncertainty in May 1967. It gained a magnificent new Eden Chapel at its junction with Fitzroy Street, dedicated 1982, which replaced the old building needed for the Grafton Centre redevelopment.

James Street: "Another of those little Victorian streets with which Cambridge is so amply endowed. Neat and solid in appearance but with nothing much to catch the eye, it leads off the busy Newmarket Road into the heart of the Fitzroy Street area. Nearly everyone agrees that it has seen few changes to date, but, depending on Whitehall decisions, this may well be a different matter in the future," So said the *News* in May 1964, when one of the newspaper's vans found a rare parking space there. James Street was then home to Frederick Morley & Co, pawnbrokers, T. Leverington grocer, greengrocer and turf commission agent, H. J. Hall chimney sweep. Opposite was the Co-operative Society's club and institute. The manager of Morley's, C.J. Fordham, recalled in 1964: "Monday morning used to be very busy and we often had queues waiting outside to put their Sunday clothes in pawn for another week…" The decline was due to the fact that many houses had been pulled down in the area and population who might have used the facilities had left district, he commented.

Concerts and protest marches were organised against the comprehensive development plans for the area. "The Kite, Cambridge's own infant breakaway state, gave a further demonstration of its 'freedom' on Saturday when a colourful procession beat the bounds of the two-day old 'city'. Led by the self-proclaimed 'Lord Mayor', 76-year-old Arthur Sutton, resplendent in red robes and riding in a two-wheeled carriage drawn by a Shire horse, some 80 'citizens' of the Kite paraded round the area boundaries which are marked by fresh green posters. The picture shows his procession in Newmarket Road." (*News*, July 1978).

The planning debate dragged on for years. Laurie and McConnal, described in 1976 as a "delightfully unrushed family department store, with free parking and a delightful restaurant", closed in 1977. Here, its empty shop still dominates Fitzroy Street in 1978. Nearby is The Talk of the Town – "not so much a department store as lots of chic mini stores under the same roof – the biggest thing to happen to the Kite shopping scene recently." (*News*, June 1978).

Laurie's distinctive bandstand was retained in the redevelopment scheme for the area, which was approved soon afterwards. The Grafton Centre was opened by the Queen in 1984 and provided everything needed to keep up with the developing fashion trend. Punks outside the new centre commented: "We're comfortable in these clothes. We don't want to wear flared trousers what you trip over in. And it means something."

Large crowds in the run-up to Christmas 1987. The Centre was extended in April 1995 to provide "a new era in Cambridge shopping" with an extra 100,000 square feet of new retail space.

In 1999 came further plans for an expansion which might transform the now pedestrianised Burleigh Street still further, bicycles having replaced parked cars by February 1987.

Around Town

The Castle area and New Chesterton

"Castle Street has undoubtedly changed over the years, more and more cottages are being demolished and more and more traffic rumbles up and down the hill. This is something some of the inhabitants find a little troublesome and many would like to see the heavy traffic take an alternative route. But in spite of new faces that have appeared, the new shops and houses, the modern street lamps, the bus service and the county buildings, the street has retained a character all its own." *News*, November 1962. Looking down Castle Hill with the Castle Inn on the left and Castle Street Methodist Church on the right middle.

The Castle mound provides the backdrop to a County Council "at home", a gathering of councillors when all disputes were to be put aside. It was June 1962, at a time when the City hoped (forlornly) it would soon be granted full county borough status. Almost inevitably a short sharp shower sent the 500 councillors scurrying for shelter in the large marquee.

From the top of Castle mound, a view over a jumble of houses to the Mount Pleasant area in August 1968.

A higher vantage point supplies the view looking down on the Pound Hill and Shelley Row in June 1976. Bottom left is St Peter's Church. After decades of neglect, the Mount Pleasant area has now been transformed by new buildings.

"There must be fewer people living in Northampton Street at present than at any time during the last 300 years. Every other house stands empty, waiting for the particular college which owns it to finally settle its future. Historically and architecturally it is a street of some interest, yet it is difficult to find anyone with really deep feeling about it and in the future this is likely to be even more true." (*News*, June 1963).

The area's story is recorded at the Folk Museum which, for many years, was administered by Enid Porter. She is seen here with a dulcimer, made in 1886 at Haslingfield by George Willmott Lawrence.

Even residents of Storey's House were seeking some relief from the summer heat in 1976.

"Today, the residential characteristics of Gloucester Street are rapidly disappearing as more and more of the cottages are falling into decay and being demolished." The County Library occupied premises formerly used as Sindall's. It housed administration and accommodated the Welfare Department, Weights and Measures, and County Library Office. Photographed in 1964.

The Shire Hall site has been extensively rebuilt, now providing the Castle Park business sites on an area which, in January 1983, housed council departments.

Beyond Huntingdon Road "is becoming increasingly popular with the University while another noticeable aspect is the number of agricultural research units and institutes it accommodates. It is a busy road, lined for most of its length with pleasant detached houses and, apart from the volume of noisy traffic it has to carry, must rank as one of the most convenient and attractive roads in which to live in Cambridge." (June 1963). In November 1985, four-star petrol was £1.92 a gallon.

Magrath Avenue, behind Shire Hall, was home to the Rex cinema and ballroom, providing an entertainment centre not only for local residents but for those from further afield, which added to the parking problems in the area when this picture was taken in October 1968. The building had opened as a roller skating rink in 1909 but was soon converted to a cinema. In 1919 it became the Rendezvous and ballroom until destroyed by a fire in 1931. It arose as an 800-seater cinema, was enlarged in 1935 and renamed the Rex in 1936. In 1954 it made national headlines when it showed the film *The Wild Ones* starring Marlon Brando, which had been banned by many cinemas. From 1967-70 it was used as a bingo hall and night-club, then became the Abbey Sports Club but closed suddenly in 1972 and was pulled down in September 1979.

In Clare Street, generations met for a great gathering at the time of the Queen's Silver Jubilee in 1977. The street party was organised by a committee from the Blackamoor's Head public house and people from neighbouring streets were invited. There were trestle tables down the middle of the street, a slap-up tea and fancy dress competition for the children, a tug-of-war and a drawing competition. The older people sat on chairs on the pavements. "We had a lovely day," they said.

Victoria Road "…has altered little in appearance since it was developed but has seen an enormous increase in traffic, and in recent years a considerable change in residents…" (February 1963). Here roadworks add to the chaos in January 1968.

May 1972, elderly people in Victoria Road, who ran a traffic gauntlet as they crossed the road to visit the Over-60s Club or get to the Post Office for their pensions. Many who visited the West Chesterton Over-60s Club at the Congregational Church were poor-sighted or had to walk with sticks. "We have been coming here for 24 years and the traffic is getting worse and worse," said one.

Children at St Luke's Playgroup practise their trike and rocking horse-riding skills in September 1975. The playgroup was opened by Heather Richardson in 1971 and ran for 12 years. The young girl in the foreground, looking at the camera, is Michelle Evans (now Copeland) who now has a four-year old son of her own. The girl with the pinafore frock on the bike in front is Anya Nicholson.

St Luke's School just after it was opened in July 1969 by Lord Butler. Brightness and light were the keynotes, even blackboards were white. It housed 288 children. One class of children – a reception class of under-fives – had to remain in the old building because the new school was not big enough. It was to have another two-classroom wing built in a second stage.

St Luke's school is a near neighbour to the old French's windmill, which closed in 1956. Here parts of the mill are being dismantled to make the structure safe; the premises were renovated in 1986 to form the centre point of a new office development.

Back on Victoria Road in February 1963, "a road of small businesses and commercial enterprise, interspersed among rows of neat but rather uninteresting houses…" (*News*).

The dread of generations of motorists, Mitcham's Corner and more roadworks, January 1967.

An oval greyhound track surrounds Cambridge City Football Club's ground in this picture taken in 1974. To the left of the ground is the club's training ground and the dog kennels are in front of the rough hedge. Milton Road leads towards the Elizabeth Way roundabout.

The junction of Milton Road with Arbury Road in May 1963. "In the years immediately prior to the Second World War, Milton Road has been surrounded by new estates and now lies well within the city. As far as present-day traffic is concerned, the road has its fair share. On football days the road becomes lined with cars, heavy lorries use it for the Fens, and in summer months traffic making for Hunstanton streams along it." (*News*, May 1963).

Arbury and King's Hedges

"In Arbury Road, the countryside has rapidly disappeared from the doorsteps, but the city with all its amenities has come to replace it. Early residents have come to accept the newcomers and both can enjoy the benefits of one of the most up-to-date estates in the country." (*News,* November 1962). Carlton Way links the leafy development of the Gilbert Road junction, pictured here in January 1973 with the new housing of 1960s Arbury.

Campkin Road. "The most popular Arbury feature are the trees, openness and quiet…living on a spanking new housing estate is far from being a cosy bed of roses…a sense of community is not generated overnight. A survey of Arbury discloses that while snags may be quite acute, they are by no means insurmountable, given determination and resourcefulness. The Arbury estate is now more than a decade old." (*News,* December 1970).

Others spoke of "the loneliness of living on a completely artificial new housing complex; residents travel to town for increased human contact and need of identity." December 1972.

Members of the Housing Committee visit Nicholson Way, North Arbury in July 1970 when it had a population of around 6,000 in its 1,600 homes and was still expanding. They grappled with issues such as a lack of amenities like shops and a playground, which they felt left the community in a peculiar limbo.

By May 1976, the message was more upbeat: "Arbury Court boasts variety for an estate. Arbury is a modern, self-contained unit which offers local residents enough choice to satisfy the demands of everyday shopping. Bishop's supermarket dominates the scene and it is their large car park which makes it worthwhile for shoppers from a much wider radius than the Arbury estate itself, making a trip of a couple of miles and still save money. Not the least of the attractions is the fish and chip shop which continues to draw customers in from a wide area, in spite of the rising cost of potatoes. One of the town's leading radio, television and washing machine dealers is predominantly placed in the Court and there is a recently modernised hardware and general goods store, two butchers, a greengrocer, chemist's, bakery, a newsagent and two clothes shops."

"The large piece of land at the junction of Campkin Road with Arbury Road where the Arbury Amenities Association hope to see a community centre and recreation ground developed." December 1964. A community centre opened in May 1974.

"Residents on the North Arbury Estate have been complaining about the length of grass on their children's playground for four months. The council say that the grass needs a flayer mower but the only one they have is out of order." Meanwhile it provided an adventure area for 2½-year-old Nicholas Grainger and his friends in July 1973.

"The 1¼-acre Arbury Adventure Playground looks like a Wild West stockade, with tall telegraph poles visible above the high fencing and a tattered Union Jack blowing in the breeze. It lies on the northern edge of the housing estate. As many as 250 children are likely to be there during the school holidays. It was parents on the estate who got the venture going and raised the initial money. Fencing alone cost more than £1,000. Since then the City Council have helped with grants." (*News*, August 1974).

There was more fun for children when a freak storm brought flooding in Campkin Road in June 1970. On "Monsoon Day", 2¼ feet of water gushed into houses and was made worse when waves made by passing traffic pushed water back into houses that had been baled out. "As parents brought out buckets and mops, the children dived for water wings. Within minutes the road took on the appearance of a seaside carnival scene, except that it was in the centre of Cambridge's biggest housing estate, 60 miles from the nearest beach. There was even surf and breakers as heavy lorries and buses barged their way through the swirling water." (*News*).

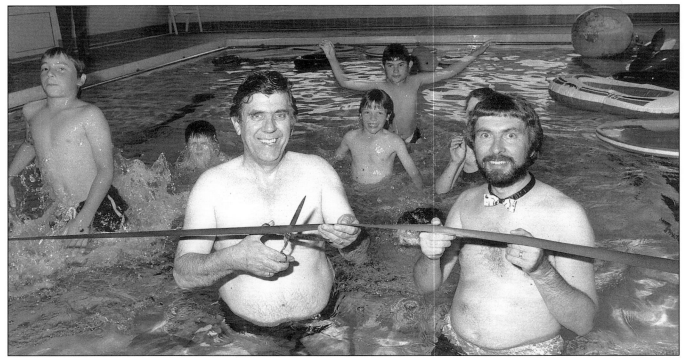

Grove Primary School gained a proper new multi-purpose swimming pool in June 1989, allowing the school's 350 pupils, including some visually and physically handicapped youngsters, to take the plunge. It was opened by chairman of the governors, Councillor Peter Cowell, and head teacher Graham Else. The school had been rebuilt in 1985 after a fire and school bosses had been fighting for a pool since then.

Skipping games for headmaster Keith Bovair and his pupils at the Lady Adrian Special School in Courtney Way, during fund raising in July 1987.

Sports day at Arbury Primary School, Carlton Way, July 1989, also saw the retirement of Barry Jones after 13 years as head teacher.

Older pupils leave Manor School in 1976. In October 1984 the school celebrated its 25th birthday when returning pupils reminisced about life in the school in 1960. Smartly-dressed parents embarrassed their children with memories of throwing pots out of Mr Morton's room, the constant evasion of maths lessons and more. "There was a white line outside the Head's office and it used to be black from the lines of boys shuffling along it waiting to be caned – it used to make us respect the teachers and we never got up to anything really bad," recalled one dad.

A new Cambridge Regional College, off King's Hedges Road, was opened by the Queen in 1993, on land adjacent to the Northern Bypass.

It is certainly an area which has seen great change. Looking back to 1963, Erica Dimock wrote: "Histon Road residents are gradually witnessing the countryside slipping away from their doorsteps. With the Arbury Road estate not very far away, another great pocket of urbanisation has materialised. However, as many residents are newcomers to the district they feel less concerned about it than do those few elderly people who have known the road all their lives." This picture shows Histon Road, looking towards Huntingdon Road, in April 1963.

"The main change seems to have been the disappearance of acres of allotments on both sides of the road and the subsequent erection of council and private dwellings on the land thus freed. Some still remain in Histon Road. But those tenanted by members of the Chesterton Allotment Society, at the corner of Arbury Road, are likely to be intruded upon before very long." Those words were written in April 1963, but these allotments remained on 3 January 1985.

Plans were put forward for a new edge-of-town shopping development, and across the railway line Trinity College pioneered a new concept – science-based industry, with its Science Park opening in 1975 and expanding rapidly since this photograph was taken in 1978.

Chesterton

The Cambridge Northern Bypass takes shape in August 1977, here crossing Milton Road, just south of the village. In the foreground the sewage works.

When the railway line to St Ives was in operation, traffic would build up at Milton Road crossing. At other times the wide grassy verges provided convenient parking for those attending the machinery sales. This photograph was taken in 1975.

A bridge over the railway line never materialised, but a subway was constructed for cars and cyclists, although this could be subject to flooding, as here in March 1964.

The St Ives line joins up with the main line to Ely and crosses Chesterton railway bridge. Much of the open fields north of the line shown in this photograph, taken in March 1975, have now been taken for St John's Innovation Centre and the Cowley Road park and ride site. In the foreground are the houses in Long Reach Road and the Cheyney Way area.

The junction of Fallowfield and Waterside seen from the air in 1975, with Franks Lane and Anglers Way in the distance. In the foreground is the river.

But it is not always an advantage to have a riverside address – 13 hours of continual rain caused flooding to houses in May 1978 and made an island of the Fort St George public house, Midsummer Common, and also inundated areas of the Backs.

Back down to earth and even areas such as Kendal Way can experience problems with encroachment on the pavement – this time by inconsiderate drivers in February 1966. Cambridge's City Surveyor, T.V. Burrows, pointed out that the houses had been built before the Second World War, when there were fewer cars on the roads and that the council was considering allowing cars to be parked in front gardens, although this could be regarded as injurious to the estate's amenities.

Shirley School pupils take advantage of the service of a "lollipop lady" in June 1964. Opened in 1932, the school was the first with up-to-date nurseries for infants, but pupils were still in wartime prefabricated buildings in 1988.

Chesterton Preparatory School pupils shortly before the school's closure in July 1972 with the retirement of headmistress, Miss Dorothy Hodder. It had opened in "temporary" buildings in 1910 and for over 60 years young children aged from three to 11 learnt their lessons – of country matters, of hedgehogs, squirrels, birds and water voles – from these premises at the bottom of De Freville Avenue. Here the children practise their maypole dancing for their final performance.

Pupils at St Andrew's School, High Street, Chesterton, celebrate the end of term in July 1981. It was the end of an era, too, for their old school, which was built in 1844, was being closed down and replaced by a new one in Nuffield Road.

A quiet moment in Chesterton High Street in May 1963. "It has very little visual attraction, few places of interest and not even a very clear identity. Its residents seem perfectly happy with it as it is, and in some respects have retained the characteristics of villagers even more than those in Cherry Hinton."

"Usually the volume of traffic in Chesterton High Street is excessively heavy along its narrow, twisting path." (*News*). This is outside the Co-op in 1964.

Hallens, corner of Union Lane, showing the air vent of the old Premier Dance Hall against the skyline in the centre. About 1925, the East Chesterton Conservative Association set up its HQ near the High Street corner of Union Lane from where it organised the activities of the Premier Dance Hall and roller skating rink next door. The property was eventually sold to a Cambridge man named Marsh and finally acquired by Mr L. W. Hallen in 1937. Parts of the old dance hall were incorporated into the development of the garage. By 1999 the whole site was being redeveloped.

Chesterton Priory has survived, but was surrounded by modern flats, here being built in 1965.

Chesterton Church, ringed by some of the buildings of the Pye company, which built its factory in Cam Road in 1913. The firm diversified into scientific instruments and televisions, becoming by 1952 the largest TV manufacturer in the country. During the 1960s, Government delay over the introduction of colour television and a world recession led to a slump and the company was taken over by Philips. Since then the Pye name has been gradually phased out, although the factory was expanded in 1978.

Herbert Charles Banham started boat building in 1906 and later turned to hire craft, building up a considerable fleet which continued operating from Cambridge until 1976.

The *Viscountess Bury* was the flagship of the Banham fleet, taking passengers and parties along the Cam to Ely. The boat, which started life as an electric launch, and was chartered to the Prince of Wales, afterwards King Edward VII, is now being restored.

A private chain ferry crossed the river to Banham's Marina, pictured here in November 1964.

The chain ferry has been replaced by Elizabeth Way and the new bridge, which was opened in 1971 when this ancient bicycle was one of the first vehicles to cross.

Herbert Street, linking Chesterton Road and Milton Road, provides a peaceful place for children to play in the late 1960s.

Chesterton Road looking towards Mitcham's corner in 1963, with a miscellaneous selection of shops on the left-hand side: Susan's hair stylist, Little-go cafe, N. E. Oliver confectioner, Hugh Calvert wholesale and retail provision merchant, A. A. Francis butcher, Miss Edna Andrews ladies hairdresser, Bruce Duncan, G. P. Hawkins bakers and confectioners.

Mitcham's shop, which gives the corner its name, opened in 1909 but closed in 1977.

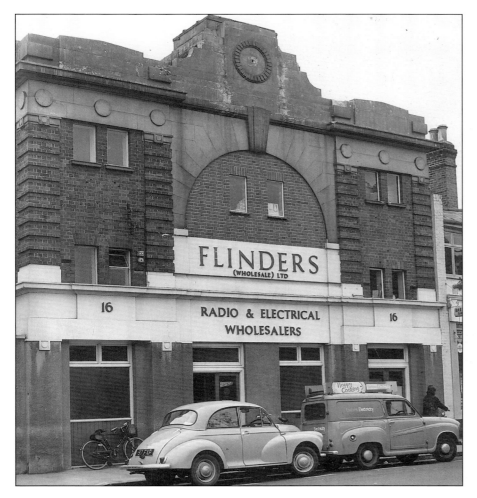

The Tivoli Cinema along Chesterton Road closed in 1956. For a while it was an electrical wholesalers, seen here in September 1963. It was subsequently converted into a fitness centre and then a pub.

"Traffic conditions at Mitcham's corner appear peaceful enough in this mid-morning aerial view. But as thousands of motorists who regularly use the junction know, conditions change radically during the early morning and late evening traffic peaks when queues of vehicles stretch for hundreds of yards along all the approach roads. Victoria Avenue, which becomes most congested of all, enters the picture on the left and links up with Chesterton Road, coming in from bottom left." (*News*). This was the scene in June 1974.

Some areas seem not to change, although motor boats are no longer allowed above Jesus Lock…

…whilst the swimming baths on Jesus Green continue to attract bathers, just as they did back in May 1966.

Newmarket Road

Chesterton is separated from Cambridge by the tranquillity of Midsummer Common: "A country scene in a town setting: cows on Midsummer Common remain unperturbed by traffic in 1967." (*News*).

Its peace is sometimes shattered: some of more than 12,000 people who packed Midsummer Common for a fireworks festival on 5 November 1983. This annual event, a replacement for the annual Guy Fawkes' battles which used to take place in the town centre in the 1960s, was initiated by the Cambridge Round Table in 1973 at Cambridge United's football ground.

Midsummer Common is home to the city's Midsummer Fair, here proclaimed in June 1983 by Mayor Betty Suckling with Mayoress Hazel Halter and the President of the Showman's Guild, Billy Whitelegg. Sergeant at Mace, Ken Quick, is on the right.

After the Lord Mayor's show… "There was Len, sweeping along Maid's Causeway, when up came this chap with a notebook and stopwatch. It took Mr Hutt back a bit. People often stop to ask him the way, but this man said he wanted to see how a road cleaner went to work. It wasn't the same. Len swept on, just as usual, with No.15 dustcart right behind, but how could a road sweeper feel relaxed with that efficiently neatly-dressed 'works study assistant' watching every sweep? It's all part of Cambridge City Council's plan to increase the efficiency of their refuse collection service. They have called in a work study firm for advice." (*News*, September 1966).

Four Lamps roundabout, June 1964, where traffic leaves the leafy Victoria Avenue for its journey into the industrialised area of Cambridge. "People grumble about the amount of traffic it has to carry and complain that it is not the most attractive of approach roads to Cambridge." (*News*).

The section of Newmarket Road between James Street and Christ Church, pictured in January 1973 before the Kite area redevelopment, showing Burchnell's auto electrical engineers and car spares.

Opposite was the Star Brewery, the only brewery still operating in the city of Cambridge by 1963. It supplied about 100 public houses in the district.

The Star Brewery continued brewing beer until June 1972. Much of the equipment was old and needing replacing, and James Ritchie, the head brewer, was retiring. Tollemache, its owners, decided to concentrate all brewing in Ipswich. The premises continued to be used as a bottling store until its closure and redevelopment for housing in 1981.

The *News* moved, in April 1962, to state-of-the-art new premises on Newmarket Road, from which the paper celebrated its centenary in 1988, before moving to larger and even more modern premises at Milton in 1994.

The corner with Wellington Street, where Finbow's removal vans shared the former Primitive Methodist Tabernacle. The firm had moved to Newmarket Road in 1940 and left in 1977. The Tabernacle, "a building of unremitting dreariness", according to Chris South, was turned into the Carioca Nightclub and Disco in 1978 with a restaurant, games room and bar billiards for a membership charge of just over 10p a week. It was devastated by a fire in September 1983.

The area had changed completely by November 1992.

The peaceful Walnut Tree Avenue, leading from Newmarket Road down to the river, in March 1964 was demolished to make way for Elizabeth Way, which opened in 1971.

The convenience of an underground toilet, at the junction with East Road, June 1968.

The previous picture contrasts with a similar view as traffic rumbles along the dualled Newmarket Road from the East Road roundabout in September 1987.

"It was in 1910 that Mr J. H. Cooper started touring the villages with his horse and cart, loaded high with all sorts of odds and ends. The business expanded until the present situation has been reached in which the Coopers occupy a considerable stretch of property opposite the Fire Station and Coldham's Lane junction. Dealing in new and second-hand furniture, the business is now run by Messrs John and Ernest Cooper and the little enterprise has reached the third generation." (*News*, July 1963).

West's garage had undergone considerable change by 1977. It started back in 1926 when Sidney West and his wife opened their first garage in Gloucester Street. After a series of moves, they opened new showrooms in Newmarket Road in March 1960, which have been updated at various times since.

Turning into Coldham's Lane in 1987 as new development continues.

Looking down on the junction in February 1966. In the background are the old industrial units, warehouses and pits off Coldham's Lane.

The area off Coldham's Lane has been redeveloped into retail parks, such as the Co-op's Beehive Centre, which opened in November 1974 as a wholesale grocers, selling to the public. It attracted large crowds and was then converted to a traditional retail outlet.

Similar plans were announced for Duce's Tip. In November 1963, the *News* reported: "A London development company wants permission to build a new suburban shopping centre with a two-storey supermarket, a garage and petrol filling station with car showrooms on the Duce's Tip site between Coldham's Lane and Newmarket Road on the lines of an American 'out of town' shopping centre for motorists…the site includes premises now occupied by Cambridge Caravans, Cook's garage and Hamptons." There was fear of the enormous volume of traffic this would attract and that it would draw off shoppers from the projected Lion Yard.

Across Newmarket Road, the Gas Works, which dominate the area in this photograph, ceased production in 1969. "The area consists of prime plots of pre-war and Victorian properties. It is the only main road development area of any size left in the city. It takes in five pubs, two banks, two tyre depots, a garage, several shops, offices and small businesses, many of which have already been approached by developers." (*News*, September 1979).

Cheddars Lane Museum of Technology, based in the old sewage pumping station, attracts crowds to its exhibits. Here in 1974, a young Timothy Chambers has a go at using the Davey valve gear of an 1894 steam pumping engine with some help from Mr Percy Lyon, the mechanic at the station.

This group of children was photographed at the Garlic Row gypsy site in 1978. Nearly 20 gypsy families who had lived for a month on waste land without sanitation or water supply were told they must move. City councillors spoke of "numerous complaints...not the right place for them to be...we want to store road building supplies there...it's the County Council's duty to provide a place for these people to stay." The gypsies replied: "Why can't they just leave us alone for a while? We don't harm anyone or cause trouble. We hardly ever leave the site."

Children train spotting at Barnwell Junction Station in 1965. In 1960 it was thriving, sending 30,000 tons of merchandise and minerals a year, including malt from Barnwell maltings. The passenger fare to Cambridge was 6d. It closed as part of the Beeching cuts.

Increasing traffic along Newmarket Road saw the replacement in 1977 of the Barnwell Road bridge, seen here in July 1963.

Barnwell Road is in the background to this aerial view of Coldham's Common, covered with caravans of people following Midsumn

The council has been fighting traffic for years. Plans for a ring road to bring traffic from Milton Road, across the river down Wadloes Road and beyond, were proposed in the 1930s. Barnwell Road was constructed but then suddenly gave way to a grass-covered kerb, a muddy track and a concrete footpath exactly 70 inches wide, seen in September 1964.

air in June 1976. The annual arrival of large numbers of such visitors caused problems.

Saturday crowds are attracted to Cambridge United's Abbey Stadium where, in 1973, some 10,542 fans set a new attendance record and experienced scenes of wild delight at the 3-2 win over Mansfield Town which saw promotion to Division Three.

Players, including United's "Footballer of the Year" Brian Greenhalgh, celebrate. Victory was secured when "Ronnie Walton burst through the Mansfield defence to hook home the winning goal and the whole of Barnwell shook with the deafening roar." (*News*).

Given such excitement, it was perhaps as well that the Ambulance Service was based at Ditton Walk. Here a crew report to base in January 1970.

More excitement for children: Residents at Ditton Fields combined to create a children's play area in 1986.

Newmarket Road, which starts with greenery, ends with greenery, thanks to Marshall's Airport, where in giant hangars the company undertake works on many civil and military schemes.

Barnwell and Romsey

Bounded by Newmarket Road, Coldham's Lane, East Road and Mill Road is an area of Cambridge which developed in the 19th century to house the large number of people who sought a new life in the expanding town of Cambridge. This area is bisected by the railway line. Across the bridge is Romsey Town, just as busy as that on the town side.

A new Sainsbury's superstore, opened in December 1974 on the corner of Coldham's Lane and Perne Road. "Traffic came almost to a standstill as queues built up; eager shoppers converged on the packed shelves and crowds formed round the plentiful supply of sugar." (*News*). The store was Sainsbury's fourth largest, with 24 twin-bay checkouts.

It adds to the competition for retailers along the Romsey Town section of Mill Road: the bustle of a busy shopping street in December 1989.

The area attracts a variety of customers to a range of shops in July 1980. Maurice and Dennis How, family bakers, completed 50 years in the bakery business in 1976. They recalled: "When we started, a large loaf cost 4d in old money; now the same loaf is 17p."

Brookfield Hospital staff, photographed in 1988. Starting life as an isolation hospital attached to Addenbrooke's, it became an old people's hospital in 1973, to nurse elderly Cambridge people near their homes. The site also provides a base for the Arthur Rank Hospice which opened in October 1981.

Romsey Junior School pupils were presented with special mugs to celebrate the 90th anniversary of their school in 1996.

Residents in Catharine Street combine to arrange an outing to the seaside in the early 1950s, an annual tradition of parties and summer outings which originated in the VE Day celebrations and lasted 25 years. Five coaches took adults and children on a seaside trip, leaving the street practically empty. The celebrations ended in 1971 when most of the original residents had left.

Increasingly, transport has switched from motor coaches to motor cars, adding to the increasing pressure of traffic. New white lines acting as a barrier from Charles Street into Stockwell Street were dubbed a "Berlin Wall" by councillors in 1967.

The railway line separates the two areas of Mill Road: to the right Great Eastern Street and Argyle Street; to the left Devonshire Road. "Lined on one side with Victorian styled terraced houses and on the other with railway goods yards, timber yards and coal depots, Devonshire Road obviously owes much of its existence to the nearness of the railway line. In spite of their close proximity to the noise and dirt of passing trains, few residents have major complaints about the road in which they live." April 1964.

The corner of Travis and Arnold's timber yard: "A large organisation of timber importers and builders merchants which covers an area from the Wash to the Bristol Channel. With its head office at Northampton, the group have nearly 1,000 employees." (*News*, April 1964).

The view from Mill Road bridge looking towards town in January 1963. The library on the right (the librarian was then Sidney Cable) closed in March 1996 despite public opposition. Beyond was Arthur Webb's hairdresser, I.B. Davies' scooter repairs, W.G. Lewis' hardware store and J. Payne's shop.

Mill Road offers a wide range of shops, like these opposite Emery Street in December 1972.

Mill Road has enjoyed a range of facilities – the Kinema, its own cinema (and bingo hall), closed in 1979. In December 1985, there were plans to restore it to its old glory, showing old time and specialist films. It would become a major tourist attraction, and shops and offices converted into a coffee bar. The plans came to nothing.

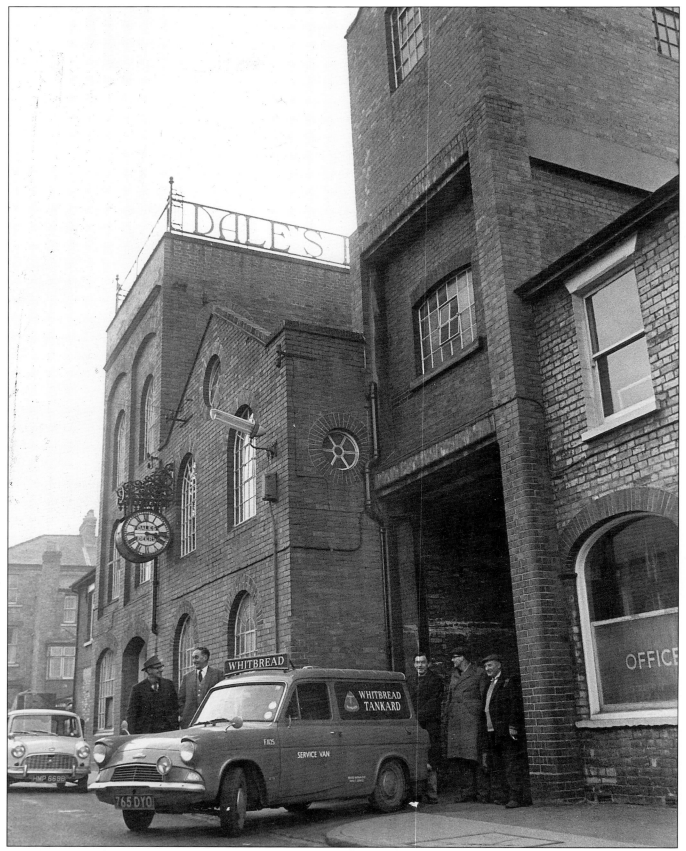

"Dale's Brewery in Gwydir Street, now used as a distribution depot for Whitbread & Co Ltd. Deliveries are made from their brewery in London and from the company's bottling depots elsewhere. They are then redistributed in the Cambridge area. Some 500 accounts, including those of public houses and off-licences, are dealt with at the Gwydir Street offices. For many years until 1961, the building was marked with a seven-foot high copper cup representing the gold cup won by Dale's for the best beers at the Brewers' International Exhibition in 1911." Those words were written in 1963. The brewery closed in 1966.

The Playhouse was demolished for a Fine Fare supermarket in 1963. It was taken over by the Salvation Army in 1985 and, as Sally Ann's, sells everything from bric-a-brac to second-hand toys and books.

The former Mill Road Union Workhouse, now Ditchburn Place, is best remembered as a maternity hospital. It was recognised in 1980 as the best in Britain, coping with 4,000 births each year.

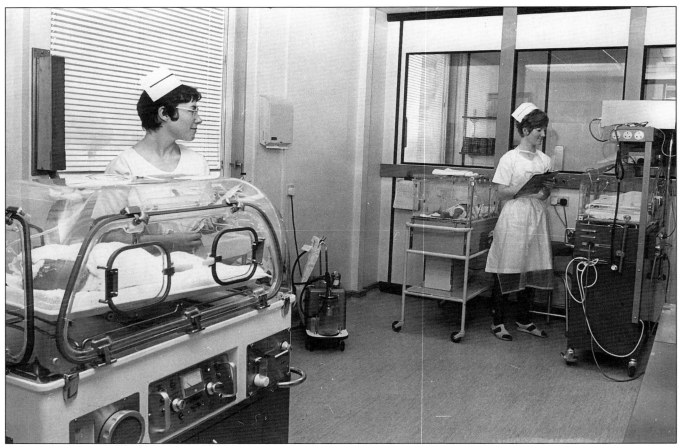

The hospital was proud of its new premature baby unit in 1969…

…but not the state of its operating theatre – a wooden shed built for the Dunkirk wounded during the Second World War. The hospital relocated to the New Addenbrooke's site in October 1983.

Other facilities also operated from wooden premises. A derelict Boy Scouts hut on the corner of Ainsworth Street and Sleaford Street was once the headquarters of the 23rd (St Matthew's) Scout troop and Wolf pack run by "Skip" Fred Feary. The building, originally erected as St James's Mission Church, had patrol rooms, table tennis and billiard rooms. Now it is a little park area with swings and seats amongst the shrubs.

Prefabricated buildings provided classrooms for students at York Street and Young Street Further Education Centre, renamed the Cambridge College of Further Education. Here in 1976 "students troop across the road from prefabs to an old church hall, getting cold and wet hourly". (*News*). It moved to Brunswick School site in 1981, before becoming part of the Cambridge Regional College which opened in new buildings on King's Hedges Road in 1993.

"It is not until one delves deep into the lesser visited streets of Cambridge that one realises just how many small industrial business there are in the city. The Abbey Street-Abbey Walk area is a good example of this, being interspersed with a miscellany of both old and more recently established firms, each making its own contribution to the trade and commerce of the district. There are signs of demolition everywhere. Bare patches temporarily used for parking cars. Abbey Street is scheduled for redevelopment for business purposes. The only shop in the road – a grocery and provisions store run by Mrs Summerlin – has been in existence for over 50 years, having previously belonged to her mother, Mrs A. Rolfe. Trade is definitely declining. Exactly what the future holds she finds hard to contemplate." These words were written in 1963, the above scene has now changed completely.

"In Abbey Walk one first comes upon the premises of Bryant and Howlett, coach builders, painters and wheelwrights. This business was founded more than 70 years ago. The firm built vans and furniture lorries from its earliest days and had the honour of producing the first commercial motor vehicle to be made in Cambridge – for G. P. Hawkins. Today (1963) Mr Bryant's work is mainly concerned with repairing and spraying old trucks and vans, and also with making wooden drop-sides for lorries, vans and other commercial vehicles." (*News*). The business has gone but this section of the street is relatively unchanged.

Sturton Street, a long narrow street of terraced houses developed in the 1870s and 1880s to house a growing population of railway workers. Since this photograph was taken in 1964, the shop has been redeveloped, the number of cars increased and young dons and professional people have made it their home.

"A number of streets in Cambridge are becoming the subjects of fairly extensive redevelopment. Norfolk Street can boast of no elegant buildings, no places of very widespread interest and no great visual interest as far as trees, gardens and open spaces are concerned…it does accommodate something getting increasingly difficult to find in Cambridge – real Cambridge characters." (*News*, December 1962).

Here in Alex Wood Hall in February 1979, council dustmen and other outdoor workers were on strike despite an 11 per cent pay increase. This seems a high percentage, but in February 1979 would have amounted to £4.50 a week extra. While the men were on strike, council environmental health officials were keeping watch on the state of 55 emergency refuse tips set up around Cambridge.

Near East Road, some streets have changed so completely that even former residents might have difficulty recognising them. This shows Staffordshire Street following 1970s rebuilding.

East Road

"Soon to become a dual carriageway and already the subject of an extensive redevelopment programme, East Road is certainly changing. It is lined for most of its length with shops and advertising hoardings, and has an atmosphere of great commercial activity. Almost invariably congested with traffic and in any case not a particularly attractive street, it is nevertheless an important one to Cambridge." *News*, June 1963.

"The extremely awkward junction which motorists have to contend with when turning into Newmarket Road from East Road." (*News*). Speechley's meat transporter van waits its turn in the queue, in June 1963.

Commanding the approach from Newmarket Road in September 1987 is the firm established in 1912 when Donald Mackay bought a small ironmonger's shop in East Road. At their Britannia Works they built up an ironmongery and engineering business. After the Second World War the company became a general engineering concern largely supplying the local building industry and contributing to various local projects. They have expanded into spiral staircases, gardening and plumbing and storage systems and are one of the few businesses to have survived on East Road.

The Cambridge Working Men's Club, on the corner of Fitzroy Street. "A shabby old East Road institution, more than beer, crib and conversation – a pool of know-how," wrote Christopher South in May 1983, just before its demolition as part of the road-widening scheme. A new building opened just along East Road in December 1984, providing a family club holding regular monthly socials, with bingo at weekends and attracting a long waiting list for membership.

Alongside, just across Fitzroy Street, A. A. Holgate's former newsagent's shop stands empty, awaiting demolition in July 1975.

By June 1963 work was already under way to make East Road a dual carriageway. The Salvation Army White Ribbon Hostel on the left provided accommodation for over 40 men, many of whom lived there permanently, paying in 1963 £3 a week for full board. Later taken over by the County Council, the facility was demolished for the Grafton Centre development. Alongside were Coulson's building works founded in 1884.

Within a year Coulson's had rebuilt their old premises and this part of the road was dualled. In 1988 they moved their operations to Cowley Road and the site became part of the new Grafton Centre extension.

By 1995 this part of East Road had changed once more as a result of the Grafton development and the arrival of new multi-screen cinemas.

Seen from the corner of Burleigh Street in 1963, "East Road is liberally scattered with the ordinary, everyday type of shop. Newsagents, confectioners, hairdressers, butchers, grocers and laundry reception offices provide local residents with everything for their immediate needs, although it is urgently in need of tidying up." (*News*, June 1963). The Baker's Arms in the middle distance – licensee in those days Mr Sidney Runham – boasted a well-used piano and a flourishing skittles club.

The Baker's Arms sign had been replaced by the time this view of the street was published in an "Ugly Cambridge" feature in the *News* in 1969. In the middle was Peak's furniture repository, originally built for storing the Cambridge Street trams that ran in the city until 1914.

The former tram sheds and shops – including Cambridge Resale, Austcott's café, the Dandelion café and K. Medcalf confectioners – seen here in August 1973. Across the road other old properties await their fate.

"It is 100 years since Mr Frederick Loker first started a newsagent's business in East Road, a business which is still being run by members of his family – two of his grandsons, Mr Denis Brown and Mr D. J. Oakman. But although Loker and Co, wholesale and retail newsagents, are known far and wide in the trade, older people will also recall the humbugs, rock and other sweets which used to be made on the premises by Mr Loker's wife and other helpers" (*News*, June 1963). In 1999, Ron Smith from Great Abington recalled: "The *Cambridge Daily News* van would pull up with the papers hot from being printed in St Andrew's Street and hand them to me to take into the shop. Mr Bilton, the butcher in Burleigh Street, gave me 2d – a penny for the paper and one for myself – for fetching it. It was a lot of money in those days, one whole penny!" The shop was photographed in November 1965. But sentiment has no place in planning and it was swept away, along with its neighbours on the corner of Norfolk Street.

Jonas Ward built bicycles from their premises on the corner of Norfolk Street but diversified into many other areas, including baby carriages. They produced their own wireless sets, were one of the first to stock televisions and sold some of the first washing machines. Ward's opened other shops and in 1965 opened a new store in Burleigh Street before closing in 1981. Their old premises became Thake's cycle shop and ended on a note of controversy when the old buildings were commandeered for a "Rave" in November 1985.

The arguments about widening the street continued. Most of the street had been dualled by 1982 as part of an urban primary route network and was used by 24,000 vehicles a day; estimates suggested this would rise to 26,000 when the Grafton Centre opened.

Behind the wire mesh fence, children of St Matthew's School faced the prospect of losing part of their playground to the road widening scheme.

In the event the scheme was shelved following protests by parents and politicians – including Anne Campbell – 1985.

The school gained new neighbours in the shape of new buildings for Cambridgeshire College of Arts and Technology, later Anglia Polytechnic University, photographed here in 1984. Trees have been planted to bring a rural touch to a very urban street.

Next door stands Zion Baptist Church and opposite this the Territorial Army Drill Hall, once a popular venue for dances and other functions, seen here in June 1963. The site has now been cleared. A plaque from it was passed to a new Territorial Army centre when it opened in Coldham's Lane in 1988.

Alongside the Drill Hall were buildings used by Cambridge University Royal Tennis Club who had four courts there before the First World War. From 1918 to 1973 it was used by Winton-Smith meats firm, famous for its cooked meats produced in the East Road factory, here photographed in 1967. It has since been replaced by the Wellington House office block.

Looking back along East Road from Gonville Place about 1969. Now even the floral roundabout has gone and the view beyond is today virtually unrecognisable.

Hills Road and New Town

Whilst the view along East Road is one of bustle, the view from the junction with Gonville Place is of tranquillity. This picture was taken in September 1963.

This can be an illusion soon shattered: "Despite a heavy increase in traffic and the fact that one side of Gonville Place is almost entirely marked out for parking, no one can deny that the outlook from this particular Cambridge Street is very attractive. In the background is the servicing and repair department of Turner and Hore's Regent Street garage. There has been a garage on this site for most of this century, previously it belonged to Mr Edward T. Saint. Today its owners are agents for BMC and Alvis vehicles, it has a petrol station on the corner and a showrooms a few yards away." (*News*, October 1963).

Both police and fire stations are situated on the corner of Parkside, where fire controllers in October 1964 are ready for action.

November 1988: Just in case something should go wrong during experiments at Parkside School. During rebuilding work the old air raid shelters were discovered in the school grounds.

Skating on Parker's Piece in February 1963 with the University Arms Hotel in the background. The final days of December 1962 saw heavy snowstorms and by early January, 400 workmen were fighting to keep traffic moving through snowdrifts. By 14 January there was skating on the Cam and people biked along the river to Grantchester. On 21st the city police station was turned into a temporary boarding house for 13 people cut off by a blizzard which piled snow into long drifts. Next day temperatures were so low that buses ground to a halt as their diesel pipes froze, as did the city's water mains. By 29 January 1963, Parker's Piece itself was under water when the snow finally melted.

The University Arms Hotel's entrance in St Andrew's Street faces across to the old police and fire station, seen here in October 1964.

From the police station, a 12-strong squad of motor-scooter police could be despatched wherever needed. The force took delivery of its first eight Vespas in June 1963.

The police scooter squad on duty at the Regal cinema to control crowds flocking to see their pop idols at the large scale tours. Diane Emmines (with basket) and Judy Gordon are among those queuing for tickets for a Beatles concert in November 1962, gently controlled by PCs Roy Coxon and Jock Urquhart.

The 1960s saw visits by many famous pop stars, like Adam Faith in March 1961.

Billy Fury meets fans Janice Bilton and Peta Truscott, 1962.

Other music was performed at the Regal cinema on its Compton organ which would rise almost majestically from the black depths of the orchestra pit between intervals in the films. Here Geoffrey Goode at the keyboard is watched by Ron Carter in 1971.

Across the road was another favourite entertainment venue – the New Theatre which closed in 1956 and was demolished in 1962. Alongside was the *Cambridge Daily News*.

Cambridge Daily News reporting staff busy at work in the days before personal computers and, indeed, even electric typewriters.

The *Cambridge Daily News* rolls off the press in St Andrew's Street. The newspaper moved to Newmarket Road in 1962.

News vendor Jock Langley, photographed in February 1966. Jock sold newspapers for 62 years from the same pitch in St Andrew's street, an old wooden hut outside the Telephone Manager's office.

Regent Street was felt in the early 1960s to be an important shopping street and one which many of its traders believed would become even more so in the future. Its prosperity, they felt, would be affected should parking meters be introduced, one trader offering to pay the charge whilst customers were in his shop.

Whether Regent Street's changing fortunes could really be attributed to traffic wardens such as Cambridge's first lady warden Mrs F. Brain, pictured here in August 1969, is uncertain.

"Cambridge stood still when the circus came to town. Elephants from Billy Smart's Circus walked from the railway station to Midsummer Common and brought traffic to a standstill." (*News*). They are pictured here in Hills Road on 24 May 1971.

Shoppers further along Hills Road seem quite oblivious to the thought of obtaining milk from bulls as the shop sign might suggest.

Russell Street: "Another of those narrow Victorian streets in the New Town area which is destined for far-reaching change within the next few years, Russell Street has little to distinguish it from other roads, apart from the fact that it has become the headquarters of the Advisory Centre for Education. Lined with small cottages and shops it also accommodates a school, and a public house." (*News*, August 1964).

Russell Street's blacksmith, Herbert E. Webb. Much of his work by 1964 was making springs of various types for motor vehicles and all types of general repairs. However, he also shod hundred of horses each year for local riding schools, his trade coming from far afield.

Panton Street Brewery had been established about 1869 and expanded by Bailey and Tebbutt about 1905. It was taken over in 1925 by Greene King who continued to brew "Fine Cambridge Ales" until 1957. The brewery was demolished in 1968.

The brewery chimney dominating the terraced houses in Coronation Street in April 1964. The area has since undergone radical rebuilding.

It is an area that is home to one of the country's top educational establishments, the Perse School for Girls, whose young ladies experiment in the chemical laboratory in July 1963.

But no amount of education can enable cyclists to see "One Way" notices when biking the other: "Bateman Street, distinguished by the presence of a college, a school and the University Botanic Garden. Its houses are mostly large and dignified but as they have no front gardens and no garages, the street is generally lined with cars, winter and summer, day and night." (*News*, May 1963).

Cars and other traffic along Hills Road defer for members of the Cambridge Old Contemptibles Association as they march to commemorate the 47th anniversary of Armistice Day, November 1965. The Methodist Chapel in the background has, like most of the marchers, now become just a memory.

The Mayor, Councillor Alec Molt, leads the tribute at the War Memorial in November 1978 as a two-gun salute is fired by the University Volunteer Training Corps.

Station Road, here in March 1963, was "lined for most of its length with trees. Its buildings are large and plain, set well back from the pavement. Many houses have been converted into offices and business premises". (*News*).

By February 1989 the extent of the transformation is apparent.

The railway station itself has undergone various improvements since this photograph of February 1971.

Once a common sight, steam trains were replaced first by diesel and then by electric trains in January 1987. The last regular train to leave Cambridge hauled by a steam locomotive, driven by Bertram George of Birdwood Road and fireman Ivor Wilson of Histon, left the goods sidings with just one carriage and a truck in June 1962.

An aerial view of November 1987, Hills Road in the foreground, Station Road running diagonally across the centre, its large offi

locks on one side of the road contrasting with the houses on the other. Mill Road runs across the middle.

Sometimes nothing at all moves, as in this June 1968 scene: "Carriages stand idle at Cambridge railway station yesterday when the rail strike closed the station." (*News*).

The Eastern Counties bus depot on Hills Road, pictured here in September 1963, was demolished in July 1987.

Coleridge and Cherry Hinton

Just across Hills Road railway bridge, a cattle market was established at the junction of Cherry Hinton Road, photographed here in August 1963. It survived there until the 1970s.

Farmers discuss the prospects of a sale in October 1965, when the Corn Market moved there from the Corn Exchange. When the farm machinery market was moved to Cowley Road in 1975, the cattle market declined and was closed.

Along with the cattle and sheep sales, a thriving Bank Holiday Market grew up, attracting crowds of bargain hunters, as here in 1968.

Part of the site has since been redeveloped as The Junction, where a concert by Blur was staged in January 1997.

Delighted…the fans at the Blur concert.

The Junction has provided a new entertainment facility for youngsters across the region, and is right on the doorstep of these children seen celebrating the centenary of Rathmore Terrace in 1989.

Students leave Coleridge School on 4 September 1971. The school celebrated its Golden Jubilee in 1987 when retired headmaster Freddie Kingdon OBE recalled how he set up a "garden laboratory" at the school. He bought an old bus for £7, sold the seats for £25, fitted it out with gas and electricity and turned it into the laboratory. It gave the school extra space, but it was not long before the planning authority discovered it and it had to be taken away. A proposal to close the school was announced in 1999, to the dismay of local residents.

Although students of Hills Road VI Form College prove they can organise their own dances, a Christmas Ball in 1986 sees Jane Dyson and Andrew Noble coaxed on to a rickety table by *News* photographer Eddie Collinson.

Post-war housing shortages saw the erection of prefabricated houses to provide temporary accommodation. Here are some of 40 derelict prefabs in Golding Road in September 1972 which were demolished to make way for new council housing in July 1974.

Looking down on the area in September 1974. Perne Road is on the right-hand side with the roundabout at Radegund Road and Birdwood Road in the distance. The new houses being constructed are at Tiverton Way, below them Chalmers Road. Cherry Hinton Road runs across the bottom.

The district gained a new church with the consecration of St Martin's Church, Suez Road, in 1961, here seen during a service in March 1964.

Cherry Hinton Hall has become the venue for a folk festival, attracting music lovers from across the world to listen to world-class performers, and camp and sing in its wooded park.

A new water park at Cherry Hinton: "When the City Council Parks Department began to make a thorough clear-out of the old spring opposite the Robin Hood public house, they realised it had an island in the centre. Plans for the newly-cleared area include planting of willow trees, spring bulbs and bog plants in wetter areas. The spring is the source of the brook which flows through Cherry Hinton and across to Brooks Road. For some time it has been home of weeds, rubbish and bicycle frames." (*News*, March 1969).

Cherry Hinton became part of Cambridge in 1934 but had experienced housing growth well before then: "Now much less of a High Street bordered by thatched cottages, farms and fields. Hundreds of new people are moving into the place every month, houses are shooting up like mushrooms and the countryside is rapidly disappearing." (*News*, April 1963). The view from Fisher's Lane, 1981 with the Baptist Church.

High Street Cherry Hinton "is changing beyond all recognition. The curving country lane of not so very many years ago is becoming a road of considerable residential and commercial importance to the city of Cambridge." (*News*, April 1963). Some local shops, photographed in April 1963.

Traffic approaching the Cherry Hinton level crossing in February 1969. Even in 1963, "Improvements to the High Street, by-passing the present level crossing, are planned, and if this happens part of the street may experience a return to the comparative quietness of former days. For the remainder, the future can only bring an increase in traffic, an increase in population and future envelopment in the city." (*News*). The by-pass has now arrived, together with considerably more housing.

They have, however, lost one source of contention: During wet weather "concrete cabbages" grow in Cherry Hinton area gardens and "stone-dashed cars" appear overnight in the streets. The reason for such unusual sights is the outfall from the chimney of a cement factory. "If any clothes are left out to dry overnight on washing lines, they need to be washed again in the morning because they are covered with a fine dust. If you clean your house windows and there is a little rain you have to clean them all over again." (February 1974). In 1963, the *News* reported: "The Norman Cement Works are still very much in operation and likely to remain so for another half century. Today between 80 and 90 are employed at the works which manufacture over 2,000 tons of concrete each week." The works closed in June 1987 and the chimney was demolished the following February.

Bad weather does not deter children: youngsters in Chalk Grove, off Queen Edith's Way, throw snowballs in November 1969.

In 1981 Netherhall School announced details of a £35,000 computer development project won by their pioneering use of new technology in education. The school was also being backed by Cambridge-based Acorn computers who were supplying them with 16 of their new BBC Microcomputers. Here, Andrew Chapman demonstrates the new machines to his teachers.

Queen Edith's Way curves across the centre of this aerial view, taken 1990, but the foreground is dominated by Addenbrooke's Hospital which has grown on the site since the 1960s.

The services offered by the Rosie Maternity Hospital were tested by this fine crop of pregnant nurses and midwives in March 1988. Head midwife Miss Christine Pugh said: "First it was one, then another, until week by week someone was announcing they were pregnant. We thought there must be something in the water supply."

Trumpington, Newnham and Madingley

Trumpington strives to retain its village feel. Here, four 17th-century cottages opposite the church, which were falling into decay, were restored in 1970. It had been intended to built old people's houses on site for Pemberton estate workers.

Trumpington has been an area of considerable growth. In this aerial view of August 1976 Paget Road and Byron Square are in the centre with Fawcett School on the left.

Nearby roads offer less frenetic conditions: rural tranquillity in Barrow Road, 6 May 1968.

Through tree-lined Brooklands Avenue with its fine houses is better known for "Butlins", the less than aesthetically pleasing block of Government offices, May 1966.

At the Cambridge University Press, Shaftesbury Road, in May 1966 Brooke Crutchley, the university printer, and Norman Bratt, publishing secretary, with ex-members of staff, check the text of the 10 millionth Ruby edition of the Bible. They are alongside one of six rotary presses, thought to be the first of their kind in the country.

The area is home to the Leys School whose sporting facilities do not normally include skating on the quadrangle, as in February 1963.

Trumpington Street, "the gateway to Cambridge and at its entrance the Students' Bookshop opened in 1940, one of only three such shops in the country. Nearby is the Fereday School of English covering most of what a student wishing to obtain a thorough knowledge of the English language would require. Traffic is fairly heavy at all times of the day and on most evenings lines of parked cars indicate that it is visiting time at the hospital." (*News*, October 1963).

The Fitzwilliam Museum attracts visitors from all around the world, some of whom attract attention themselves – a visit by Queen Elizabeth the Queen Mother in July 1966 to open a £90,000 extension to coincide with the 150th anniversary of the building.

Although its magnificent collections are also enhanced by visiting exhibitions – including the work of the local artists. Ashley Dell of Cambridge, Colin Eberhardt of Burwell and Natalie Thurtle of Great Bradley were winners of a children's art competition organised by the Friends of the Fitzwilliam Museum, October 1988.

"Addenbrooke's Hospital is gradually being transferred to its new home and the years ahead will no doubt be ones of progress and major importance. The future of the Trumpington Street site is still uncertain but it will not be vacated for a good many years as the second stage of development of Hills Road is not due for completion before the early 1970s." (*News*, October 1963). The first stage of the new hospital had been opened by the Queen in 1962. Old Addenbrooke's finally closed in October 1984 – the same year that a two-year old liver transplant boy, Ben Hardwick, featured on *That's Life*.

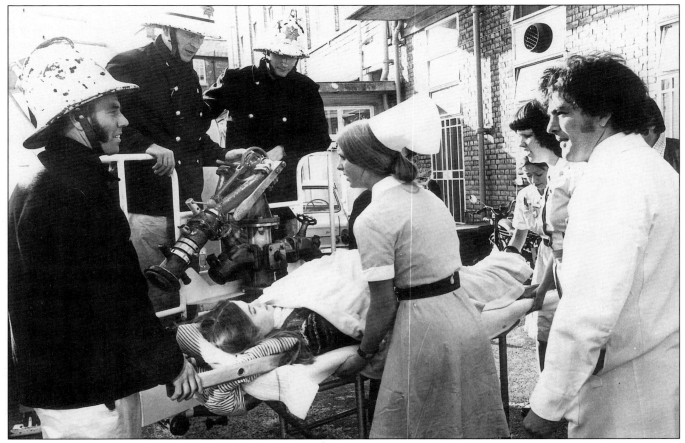

Here in 1977, staff practise evacuation in event of a fire.

Fire swept through the Garden House Hotel in April 1972. It reopened 16 months later after a £2 million rebuilding programme. Meanwhile there was pressure on hotel beds as more and more visitors swarmed to Cambridge. In 1973 the average cost of bed and breakfast in a private house in Cambridge was £2 a night, while the cost in a leading hotel was at least double that. "What we badly need is something like a hostel where people can stay at £1 a head," said staff at the tourist information bureau. "Most of the people who come to us can't afford to stay at the hotels."

Guests attending a Greek holiday promotion in July 1970 found themselves caught up in what became known as the "Garden House Riot", when a student protest against the then Greek military regime got out of hand.

Nearby, the Mill Pool provides an attractive spot for a pint or picnic, or generally watching the world go by, as here in March 1961.

If things get too hot, Newnham Pool offers a chance to cool off. This picture was taken on 13 August 1965 when temperatures soared into the 80s.

And Coe Fen, seen here in 1978, can be attractive at all seasons.

A pleasant walk under the trees of Barton Road, July 1965. "Almost entirely residential in character, Barton Road must rank as one of the most pleasant roads in which to live in Cambridge. It is convenient for most parts of the city and university, only a short distance from the open country and carries no excessive amount of traffic. Unlikely to be altered to any great extent in the future, it is not surprising that its inhabitants are so obviously content," said the *News*.

Pupils of Newnham Croft Primary School in 1985 were experiencing overcrowded classrooms, leaky roofs, mildew and outdated lavatories. The prefabricated school dining hall was demolished in 1982 because it was unsafe and so children had to bring packed lunches to eat in class. A new school opened in March 1990 with new classrooms, kitchens and community facilities.

Unanticipated by *Down Your Street* compiler, Erica Dimock, in 1963 was the growth in new colleges that the next 30 years would bring. Here houses at the Grange Road end of the site are demolished in February 1977 for the new Robinson College.

New buildings of Churchill College prove a happy picking place for a two-year-old Alexandra Double – until she met college porter Mr W. Mercer, but "she has a winning smile, so every thing was all right this time," *News*. In March 1969 the college became the first to agree to admit women students to a men's college. The first woman undergraduate, Mrs Vanessa Dowell, was admitted in October 1972.

Even further out into the countryside, Vicar's Farm on Madingley Road was earmarked as part of the University "West Cambridge" science site which has since developed into a major addition to the University's facilities.

University and Colleges

Tourists are attracted to Cambridge less by the excellence of the science than by the grandeur of the architecture – here glimpsed beyond wire-mesh barricades from the top of Great St Mary's Church in October 1972.

Inevitably tourism brings difficulties for those who live and work in the colleges. Restrictions have been imposed and charges introduced.

A Blue Badge Guide gives visitors an authorised version of the University's history in April 1974.

They need to keep up to date, even within the historic centre. The University and colleges have expanded greatly over the last 30 years. Here C. T. Cripps and his party, (Revd J. S. Boys Smith, Master of St John's is on the left) make their way to tea after the opening of the new St John's College Cripps building, May 1967.

There is no telling who one might bump into in the street – Prince Charles walking back to his college rooms after beginning the final examination for his Bachelor of Arts degree in May 1970.

The Duke of Edinburgh in more formal robes, as Chancellor of the University, in Market Hill, June 1979.

The Master of Trinity College, Lord Butler, perched on the fountain in the middle of Great Court in August 1967, when the clock sounded two in the afternoon with four chimes. It was on the occasion of the college's annual Caucus Race when undergraduates in academic and other bizarre costume walked and ran round the 18 rectangles formed out of the Court's six grassed areas. It seemed something out of Wonderland – but isn't that what Cambridge is all about anyway?

Elsewhere in Trinity College, *News* photographer records the scene as students sign the college admissions book, and are then photographed by the Sub Librarian, Mr A. Halcrow for college records, 1967.

Occasionally film and television cameras bring the activities to millions – the Christmas Eve service from King's College Chapel in December 1990 featured the voices of Magnus Johnston, Dominic Gill, Peter Winn and Graeme Gordon.

A televised debate at the Union Society, October 1964, when MP Gerald Nabarro told undergraduates: "The Tories have no knowledge about the working classes, and the Socialists are mere gold-watch trained Trades Union members." Mr Norman Lamont, of Fitzwilliam House, said that if one had grown tired of the politics, the personalities proved just as interesting.

Here the building is used for quite another event: "The prospect for chair-borne judges in the Union Society cellars at the preliminary round of the Cambridge University Rag Queen contest, November 1967," *News*. This is one "tradition" that has now died out.

Rag Day itself is one which has had mixed fortunes; "A charming highwayman uses her powers of persuasion on an early morning motorist." (1972).

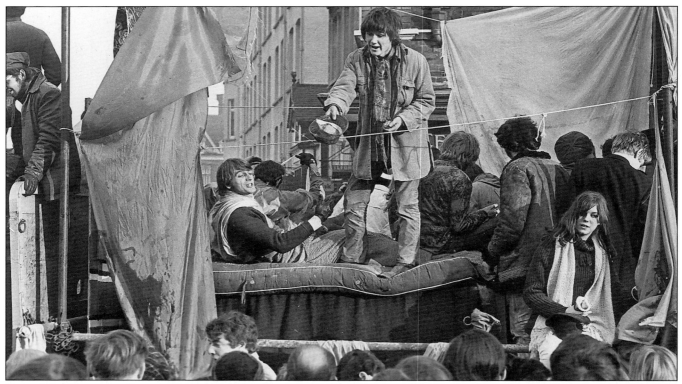

Part of the Rag procession, probably 1967. The first organised procession of floats started in 1963, raising money for the Earl Haig appeal, as they had since 1922. But shortly afterwards everything seemed to fall apart. Although in 1965 the students sold out of poppies, many colleges boycotted the event, wanting some of the money to go to other groups as well. In 1967 the traditional "Poppy Day" rag was held for the last time. In 1969 the date was changed to February but the event was a flop with few stunts. It enjoyed a revival and in 1980 the organisation was taken over by the Cambridge Students Union and takings soared.

New stunts are tried from time to time: Trinity College undergraduates, with help from the women's colleges, attempting to cram 27 people into a Mini car, part of Rag Day, February 1969.

But old traditions predominate: The May Week celebrations still continue to mark the culmination of the University year. Here guests at the 1969 Pembroke May Ball meet and relax between dances during the evening.

A major change in University life has been the admission of female students to all colleges. Some still ban men. Here Queen Elizabeth the Queen Mother chats to domestic staff at the opening of New Hall in 1965, one of the few remaining women-only colleges.

The hard academic work culminates in the award of degrees at the Senate House, usually with the mums and dads, maters and paters, of successful students looking on in admiration, as here. The situation was reversed in 1999 when ladies who had studied in Cambridge before the Queen Mother became the first woman to be awarded a Cambridge University degree, returned to the Senate House for a special ceremony and the accolade of their children and grandchildren. The struggle for full recognition had been a long one.

Not all who wear academic gowns are content. In May 1969 students set fire to gowns on the Senate House lawn in protest against having to gear their studies to examinations. The Senior Proctor called it: "The usual type of rather silly protest." The requirement for students to wear gowns in the streets after dusk had been abolished in 1965.

The abolition of the law about gowns reduced the work of the Proctors and Bulldogs – the University law enforcers, seen here in April 1965.

They were in the front line, however, when in February 1973 1,000 students, seeking greater participation in running the University, marched on the Old Schools, which the previous year had been occupied in protest against reform of examinations.

Heavy rain dampened passions in February 1973 when an anticipated 1,000 participants were reduced to just 300, some of whom gathered on King's Parade to protest about changes in student grants.

The same issue – but different fashions in November 1989 when a rally of 1,000 students in protest at Government proposals to change the way student grants were funded had the support of the University Vice Chancellor. The protest banners urged "Save the whale", and "Parents don't have brainy kids – they cost too much."

In November 1976 it was University staff who did have kids and battled for the provision of nursery and creche facilities who demonstrated outside the Senate House. Inside dons were debating a report supporting the proposal at a cost of £16,000 a year.

At other times the protests have been more political – banners proclaiming "US out of Vietnam", "Don't railroad the Unions", "Expand education for all", are pictured in Market Street.

Inside the Guildhall in 1970, General Election candidates David Lane (Conservative) and George Scurfield (Labour) chat during the count. Lane retained the seat he had won at a by-election in 1967, with a majority of just over 5,000 votes. Local government results can be swung by University voters.

When it all gets too crowded in the city centre – as on King's Parade during Rag Week, February 1976…

...one can always escape to the peace of the Backs – although not in May 1963, when the University Madrigals brought hundreds of members of both Town and Gown to the banks of the Cam.

Not even the Backs can be guaranteed exemption from the intrusion of the motor car – an Austin suspended under the Bridge of Sighs, 1963.

Generally, however, there is relative tranquillity, and for millions this is the memory of Cambridge they carry with them – punting on the river in April 1964.

Or just maybe actually walking on the river, as here in February 1963, in this city for all seasons.